5 minutes to calm

5 minutes to calm

create daily peace in 52 mindful and meditative ways

Tania Ahsan

SIRIUS

All images courtesy of Shutterstock.

SIRIUS

This edition published in 2022 by Sirius Publishing, a division of
Arcturus Publishing Limited,
26/27 Bickels Yard, 151–153 Bermondsey Street,
London SE1 3HA

ISBN: 978-1-3988-0880-5
AD008600US

Printed in China

Introduction

This is your journal. This is the five minutes in your day that are yours alone. You can either choose to write in it first thing in the morning or last thing at night or when the children are napping or when you're lying in the bath... in short, whenever and wherever you can find five minutes to bring some calm into your daily routine.

Don't make this another chore or something to add to your "to do" list. The pages here are designed to inspire you to think about the wonderful things in your life and to remember with gratitude how many things keep going right. If a suggestion doesn't resonate with you, ignore it and turn to a blank page to write freely about anything you like. Or draw something. Or doodle in a relaxed state of mind. If a page suggests you list some things, don't feel you have to write out answers for the exact number of spaces given—you may only have two, in which case, draw yourself a nice picture on the rest of the page. If you have more than the numbers given, use another page to continue your thoughts. Calm comes when you realize that you are in control. Don't allow fear or expectations to rob you of your peace of mind. Enjoy your day... and remember you're in charge!

Tania Ahsan

Your week ahead

Affirmation of the week: *I am enough.*

Date:
_____

What one thing will you do every day this week to instill a sense of calm?

_____
_____
_____
_____

What do you like most about yourself? This week showcase that quality through your actions.

_____
_____
_____

Which three people will you make a real effort to be kind to this week?

1. _____

2. _____

3. _____

How did it go?

When did you feel most calm this week?

_____

_____

_____

_____

How did you celebrate the quality you like most about yourself?

_____

_____

_____

_____

How did you show kindness to your three chosen people? What was their response?

_____

_____

_____

_____

Is there anything that could have gone better this week?
How would you have acted differently?

_____

_____

_____

_____

Delicious memories

Which foods make your toes curl with pleasure? Are there happy memories associated with them? Could you make or buy them this week?

Your week ahead

Affirmation of the week: *I am serene.*

Date:

What one thing will you do every day this week to instill a sense of calm?

_____

_____

_____

_____

Who is your role model? This week try to emulate the person you admire the most.

_____

_____

_____

_____

Which three people will you make a real effort to be kind to this week?

1. _____

2. _____

3. _____

How did it go?

When did you feel most calm this week?

_____

_____

_____

_____

How did you emulate your role model?

_____

_____

_____

_____

How did you show kindness to your three chosen people? What was their response?

_____

_____

_____

_____

Is there anything that could have gone better this week?
How would you have acted differently?

_____

_____

_____

_____

Your week ahead

Affirmation of the week: *I am relaxed.*

Date:

What one thing will you do every day this week to instill a sense of calm?

What one thing can you delegate to someone else? This week pick one thing you can get help with, either at home or at work.

Which three people will you make a real effort to be kind to this week?

1.

2.

3.

How did it go?

When did you feel most calm this week?

What did you delegate? Was the person to whom you delegated happy to help?

How did you show kindness to your three chosen people? What was their response?

Is there anything that could have gone better this week?
How would you have acted differently?

How do you feel right now?

Write or draw what you're feeling at this exact moment.

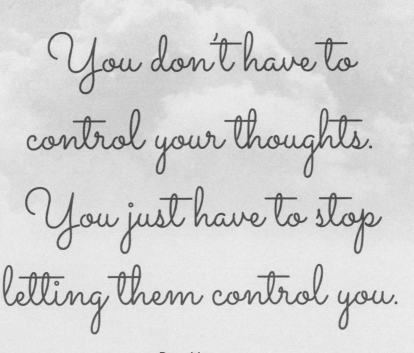

You don't have to control your thoughts. You just have to stop letting them control you.

DAN MILLMAN

Your week ahead

Affirmation of the week: *I am vibrant.*

Date:

What one thing will you do every day this week to instill a sense of calm?

What physical activity makes you feel most like yourself? This week go and enjoy some movement and then enjoy being still afterwards.

Which three people will you make a real effort to be kind to this week?

1.

2.

3.

How did it go?

When did you feel most calm this week?

_____

_____

_____

_____

Which physical activity did you choose? How did it feel both during and afterwards?

_____

_____

_____

_____

How did you show kindness to your three chosen people? What was their response?

_____

_____

_____

_____

Is there anything that could have gone better this week?
How would you have acted differently?

_____

_____

_____

_____

_____

Your week ahead

Affirmation of the week: *I am cheerful.*

Date:

What one thing will you do every day this week to instill a sense of calm?

What cheers you up? This week visit folks who make you happy or watch films and shows that bring a smile to your face.

Which three people will you make a real effort to be kind to this week?

1.

2.

3.

How did it go?

When did you feel most calm this week?

_____

_____

_____

What cheered you up this week?

_____

_____

_____

_____

How did you show kindness to your three chosen people? What was their response?

_____

_____

_____

_____

Is there anything that could have gone better this week?
How would you have acted differently?

_____

_____

_____

_____

Your week ahead

Affirmation of the week: *I am composed.*

Date:

What one thing will you do every day this week to instill a sense of calm?

Consider responding with composure and calm when you next encounter an annoyance. This might feel strange to do, but pause before you react calmly.

Which three people will you make a real effort to be kind to this week?

1.

2.

3.

How did it go?

When did you feel most calm this week?

_____

_____

_____

_____

Which annoyance did you meet calmly? Did you feel better about the situation?

_____

_____

_____

_____

How did you show kindness to your three chosen people? What was their response?

_____

_____

_____

_____

Is there anything that could have gone better this week?
How would you have acted differently?

_____

_____

_____

_____

Your week ahead

Affirmation of the week: *I am gentle.*

Date:

What one thing will you do every day this week to instill a sense of calm?

Where in your life can you show gentleness? This softness is not a weakness, but a considerable strength.

Which three people will you make a real effort to be kind to this week?

1.

2.

3.

How did it go?

When did you feel most calm this week?

Where did you show gentleness this week? How did it feel?

How did you show kindness to your three chosen people? What was their response?

Is there anything that could have gone better this week?
How would you have acted differently?

Set peace of mind as your highest goal, and organize your life around it.

BRIAN TRACY

How do you feel right now?

Write or draw what you're feeling at this exact moment.

Your week ahead

Affirmation of the week: *I am full of wonder.*

Date:

What one thing will you do every day this week to instill a sense of calm?

When do you feel a sense of awe and wonder? This week get out to those landscapes that make you feel like the world is enchanted and magical.

Which three people will you make a real effort to be kind to this week?

1.

2.

3.

How did it go?

When did you feel most calm this week?

_____

_____

_____

Which wonder-filled landscape did you visit? What did it reawaken in you?

_____

_____

_____

How did you show kindness to your three chosen people? What was their response?

_____

_____

_____

Is there anything that could have gone better this week?
How would you have acted differently?

_____

_____

_____

_____

Your week ahead

Affirmation of the week: *I am still.*

Date:

What one thing will you do every day this week to instill a sense of calm?

Where can you stop and be still? This week give yourself space to just be.

Which three people will you make a real effort to be kind to this week?

1.

2.

3.

How did it go?

When did you feel most calm this week?

How did you find a place of stillness in your week?

How did you show kindness to your three chosen people? What was their response?

Is there anything that could have gone better this week?
How would you have acted differently?

Worries Float Away

Write out a single word for a worry you have on each of the balloons opposite. Now close your eyes and imagine those worries floating away until you can no longer see them. How does it feel to know your problems have floated away?

Your week ahead

Affirmation of the week: *I am blessed.*

Date:

What one thing will you do every day this week to instill a sense of calm?

Where in your life do you feel particularly blessed? This week enjoy your blessings and don't take them for granted.

Which three people will you make a real effort to be kind to this week?

1.

2.

3.

How did it go?

When did you feel most calm this week?

_____

_____

_____

_____

In which way did you feel blessed this week?

_____

_____

_____

_____

_____

How did you show kindness to your three chosen people? What was their response?

_____

_____

_____

_____

_____

Is there anything that could have gone better this week?
How would you have acted differently?

_____

_____

_____

_____

_____

_____

Your week ahead

Affirmation of the week: *I am wise.*

Date:

What one thing will you do every day this week to instill a sense of calm?

Which words of wisdom have stayed with you? This week show your understanding of those words by following that advice.

Which three people will you make a real effort to be kind to this week?

1.

2.

3.

How did it go?

When did you feel most calm this week?

_____

_____

_____

_____

How did you bring wisdom into your life this week?

_____

_____

_____

_____

How did you show kindness to your three chosen people? What was their response?

_____

_____

_____

_____

Is there anything that could have gone better this week?
How would you have acted differently?

_____

_____

_____

_____

How do you feel right now?

Write or draw what you're feeling at this exact moment.

Be like a tree and let
the dead leaves drop.

RUMI

Your week ahead

Affirmation of the week: *I am comfortable.*

Date:

What one thing will you do every day this week to instill a sense of calm?

What does it mean to be comfortable? This week think about all the ways in which comfort is a part of your life—physical, financial, emotional.

Which three people will you make a real effort to be kind to this week?

1.

2.

3.

How did it go?

When did you feel most calm this week?

_____

_____

_____

_____

How did you invite more comfort into your life this week?

_____

_____

_____

_____

How did you show kindness to your three chosen people? What was their response?

_____

_____

_____

_____

Is there anything that could have gone better this week?
How would you have acted differently?

_____

_____

_____

_____

_____

Your week ahead

Affirmation of the week: *I am joyful.*

Date:

What one thing will you do every day this week to instill a sense of calm?

What gave you joy when you were a child? This week revisit that happiness by doing that activity, even if you feel a little silly doing it.

Which three people will you make a real effort to be kind to this week?

1.

2.

3.

How did it go?

When did you feel most calm this week?

_____

_____

_____

_____

How did you revive the joy you felt as a child?

_____

_____

_____

_____

How did you show kindness to your three chosen people? What was their response?

_____

_____

_____

_____

Is there anything that could have gone better this week?
How would you have acted differently?

_____

_____

_____

_____

_____

Your week ahead

Affirmation of the week: *I am caring.*

Date:

What one thing will you do every day this week to instill a sense of calm?

How can you show your caring side this week? Draw on the quality of caring through your actions.

Which three people will you make a real effort to be kind to this week?

1.

2.

3.

How did it go?

When did you feel most calm this week?

_____

_____

_____

_____

How did you show you care this week? Did you give the gift of time and attention?

_____

_____

_____

_____

How did you show kindness to your three chosen people? What was their response?

_____

_____

_____

_____

Is there anything that could have gone better this week?
How would you have acted differently?

_____

_____

_____

_____

Your week ahead

Affirmation of the week: *I am rested.*

Date:

What one thing will you do every day this week to instill a sense of calm?

Are you getting enough rest? This week try to spend an hour before bed just winding down and relaxing.

Which three people will you make a real effort to be kind to this week?

1.

2.

3.

How did it go?

When did you feel most calm this week?

_____

_____

_____

Did you feel more rested than in other weeks? How can you continue to feel this way?

_____

_____

_____

_____

How did you show kindness to your three chosen people? What was their response?

_____

_____

_____

_____

Is there anything that could have gone better this week?
How would you have acted differently?

_____

_____

_____

_____

The nearer a person comes to a calm mind, the closer they are to strength.

MARCUS AURELIUS

How do you feel right now?

Write or draw what you're feeling at this exact moment.

Your week ahead

Affirmation of the week: *I am strong.*

Date:

What one thing will you do every day this week to instill a sense of calm?

Where do you feel strong? This week concentrate your energy on retaining a sense of your own strength—both physical and emotional.

Which three people will you make a real effort to be kind to this week?

1.

2.

3.

How did it go?

When did you feel most calm this week?

_____

_____

_____

_____

How did you celebrate your strength this week?

_____

_____

_____

_____

How did you show kindness to your three chosen people? What was their response?

_____

_____

_____

_____

Is there anything that could have gone better this week?
How would you have acted differently?

_____

_____

_____

_____

Your week ahead

Affirmation of the week: *I am friendly.*

Date: _____

What one thing will you do every day this week to instill a sense of calm?

_____

_____

_____

How can you show the world your friendliness? This week try and smile at strangers and talk to people you might not usually connect with.

_____

_____

_____

Which three people will you make a real effort to be kind to this week?

1. _____

2. _____

3. _____

How did it go?

When did you feel most calm this week?

_____

_____

_____

_____

How was your friendliness received?

_____

_____

_____

_____

How did you show kindness to your three chosen people? What was their response?

_____

_____

_____

_____

Is there anything that could have gone better this week?
How would you have acted differently?

_____

_____

_____

_____

Your week ahead

Affirmation of the week: *I am happy.*

Date: _____

What one thing will you do every day this week to instill a sense of calm?

_____
_____
_____
_____

What does happiness mean to you? This week make a note of all things—big and small—that make you happy.

_____
_____
_____
_____

Which three people will you make a real effort to be kind to this week?

1. _____

2. _____

3. _____

How did it go?

When did you feel most calm this week?

_____

_____

_____

_____

Which aspects of life really made you feel happy this week?

_____

_____

_____

_____

How did you show kindness to your three chosen people? What was their response?

_____

_____

_____

_____

Is there anything that could have gone better this week?
How would you have acted differently?

_____

_____

_____

_____

How do you feel right now?

Write or draw what you're feeling at this exact moment.

There is never anything
but the present, and if
one cannot live there, one
cannot live anywhere.

ALAN WATTS

Your week ahead

Affirmation of the week: *I am mindful.*

Date:

What one thing will you do every day this week to instill a sense of calm?

What does it mean to be mindful? This week pay attention to your thoughts and actions and observe your way of being in the world.

Which three people will you make a real effort to be kind to this week?

1.

2.

3.

How did it go?

When did you feel most calm this week?

How did you become more mindful this week?

How did you show kindness to your three chosen people? What was their response?

Is there anything that could have gone better this week?
How would you have acted differently?

Personal Peace Planner

Which books have left you feeling joyful? Make a list of the authors and commit to either discovering new books by them or picking up one book you like the look of by an author you haven't read before.

1.

2.

3.

4.

5.

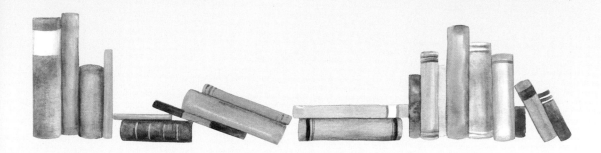

6.

7.

8.

9.

10.

Your week ahead

Affirmation of the week: *I am safe.*

Date:

What one thing will you do every day this week to instill a sense of calm?

Are you fearful and untrusting of the world around you? This week try to see if there are areas in which you could safely show more trust.

Which three people will you make a real effort to be kind to this week?

1.

2.

3.

How did it go?

When did you feel most calm this week?

_____

_____

_____

_____

Feeling physically and emotionally safe is vital in life. Did trusting more help you feel safer?

_____

_____

_____

_____

How did you show kindness to your three chosen people? What was their response?

_____

_____

_____

_____

Is there anything that could have gone better this week?
How would you have acted differently?

_____

_____

_____

_____

_____

Far horizons

Think about the last time you felt completely relaxed and at peace. Where were you? What could you smell? How did your body feel? Close your eyes and take yourself back there in your memory. Breathe in the experience.

Your week ahead

Affirmation of the week: *I am loved.*

Date:

What one thing will you do every day this week to instill a sense of calm?

There are so many more types of love than romantic—who loves you and who do you love? This week show appreciation for the love in your life.

Which three people will you make a real effort to be kind to this week?

1.

2.

3.

How did it go?

When did you feel most calm this week?

Where does love manifest in your life?

How did you show kindness to your three chosen people? What was their response?

Is there anything that could have gone better this week?
How would you have acted differently?

Loving your now

What do you love about where
you live right now?

Think about your life right now, just as it is. What do you love and appreciate about it?

Your week ahead

Affirmation of the week: *I am at peace with myself.*

Date:

What one thing will you do every day this week to instill a sense of calm?

How can you accept yourself more, even your flaws? This week bring your focus into how you can show yourself some love.

Which three people will you make a real effort to be kind to this week?

1.

2.

3.

How did it go?

When did you feel most calm this week?

_____

_____

_____

_____

How did you go about finding acceptance for yourself?

_____

_____

_____

_____

How did you show kindness to your three chosen people? What was their response?

_____

_____

_____

_____

Is there anything that could have gone better this week?
How would you have acted differently?

_____

_____

_____

_____

You yourself, as much
as anybody in the entire
universe, deserve your love
and affection.

SHARON SALZBERG

How do you feel right now?

Write or draw what you're feeling at this exact moment.

Your week ahead

Affirmation of the week: *I am kind.*

Date:

What one thing will you do every day this week to instill a sense of calm?

To whom could you be kinder—yourself, perhaps? This week find ways to show kindness to yourself as well as others.

Which three people will you make a real effort to be kind to this week?

1.

2.

3.

How did it go?

When did you feel most calm this week?

_____

_____

_____

_____

In which ways were you kind to yourself?

_____

_____

_____

_____

How did you show kindness to your three chosen people? What was their response?

_____

_____

_____

_____

Is there anything that could have gone better this week?
How would you have acted differently?

_____

_____

_____

_____

Personal Peace Planner

List the times you can remember really having a belly laugh. Who were you with? What were you doing? How old were you?

1.

2.

3.

4.

5.

6.

7.

8.

9.

10.

Your week ahead

Affirmation of the week: *I am grateful.*

Date:

What one thing will you do every day this week to instill a sense of calm?

What are you grateful for? Does gratitude help you feel less irritation when things go wrong? Look for how it makes you feel.

Which three people will you make a real effort to be kind to this week?

1.

2.

3.

How did it go?

When did you feel most calm this week?

How did gratitude help you this week?

How did you show kindness to your three chosen people? What was their response?

Is there anything that could have gone better this week?
How would you have acted differently?

Each butterfly in this picture is one of your blessings.
Count and name as many of them as you can.

Personal Peace Planner

Write down ten things you like about yourself. Think of personality traits rather than how you look. Return to this page if you need more time. Ask yourself why you need more time for this exercise and try to get to the stage where you can instantly think of many more reasons to like yourself.

1.

2.

3.

4.

5.

6.

7.

8.

9.

10.

Your week ahead

Affirmation of the week: *I am giving*.

Date:

What one thing will you do every day this week to instill a sense of calm?

Where can you give more of yourself? Without over-committing yourself, is there some way you can give back to your community?

Which three people will you make a real effort to be kind to this week?

1.

2.

3.

How did it go?

When did you feel most calm this week?

_____

_____

_____

_____

How did giving of your time feel?

_____

_____

_____

_____

How did you show kindness to your three chosen people? What was their response?

_____

_____

_____

_____

Is there anything that could have gone better this week?
How would you have acted differently?

_____

_____

_____

_____

_____

How do you feel right now?

Write or draw what you're feeling at this exact moment.

When we stop
re-reading the last chapter
of our life, we leave room
to write a new one.

TAMARA LEVITT

Your week ahead

Affirmation of the week: *I am contented.*

Date:

What one thing will you do every day this week to instill a sense of calm?

What would make you feel content? This week think about the things you need in order to feel happy in life.

Which three people will you make a real effort to be kind to this week?

1.

2.

3.

How did it go?

When did you feel most calm this week?

Did you discover the elements of what makes you happy? Do you have those things in your life now?

How did you show kindness to your three chosen people? What was their response?

Is there anything that could have gone better this week?
How would you have acted differently?